THE HEYDAY OF
LONDON'S BUSES

KEVIN McCORMACK

First published 1992
Reprinted 1994

ISBN 0 7110 2121 X

Published by Ian Allan Publishing:
an imprint of Ian Allan Ltd, Terminal House, Station Approach, Shepperton, Surrey
TW17 8AS; and printed by Ian Allan Printing Ltd Coombelands House, Coombelands Lane,
Addlestone, Weybridge, Surrey KT15 1HY.

All photographs unless otherwise credited were taken by the author.

Family Reunion
Front cover:
*West Croydon station was one of many locations around London where red
and green buses of the same type could meet. RT3461 has just arrived from
Chelsham on route 403 while RT624, later to become the last red RT to run in
public service, waits to leave for Woolwich Arsenal station on route 54.*

Silver Jubilee
Right:
*RM1648, one of 25 Routemasters specially painted to mark the Silver Jubilee of
the Queen's accession to the throne, passes the National Gallery, Trafalgar
Square, during the summer of 1977.*

IAN ALLAN
Publishing

INTRODUCTION

The Heyday of the London Bus could be attributed to various periods of history; but for me, the heyday covered the postwar era in which I grew up. This was a time when London had a standardised fleet of modern buses designed specifically for the capital's demanding traffic conditions, and carried conductors — a far cry from the subsequent generation of traffic-clogging, off-the-shelf rectangular boxes. Admittedly, the traditional London bus, in the form of the celebrated Routemaster, can still be seen in reduced numbers in the city's streets; but, for many people, the heyday period ended in 1979 when the early postwar RT double-decker and its single-decker contemporary, the RF, were withdrawn from service. The photographs in this book date mainly from the 1970s, a period of renewal for these vehicles as they enjoyed an unexpected Indian summer at the expense of the unreliable buses which were intended to replace them. Other contemporary buses, including the Routemaster, are also featured.

My interest in London buses began in childhood when I lived within earshot of the former 97 route in Ealing and started marking off the bus numbers in my Ian Allan spotting books. However, after the last trolleybus was withdrawn in 1962, the focus of my attention moved to the demise of steam trains

Dead wood

Right:
An autumnal scene is created by dying elms in Sandy Lane, Ham, as RT4412 heads for Kingston on route 71 during the summer of 1976. RTs gave way to Routemasters on 5 March 1978.

Outside Inn

Right:
On 1 January 1970, control of London Transport passed to the now defunct Greater London Council. This meant that London Transport had to relinquish its Country (green) bus and Green Line coach services to London Country Bus Services, a newly formed subsidiary of the National Bus Company. While still on LT's payroll, RF 660 creates a typical early 1950s scene outside The Vernon Arms at the Harefield, Hillend Road, terminus of route 309 in July 1969.

Outcast

Below right:
The Leyland equivalent of the AEC Regent (RT) was the Titan PD2/1. Designated RTL, these buses were the same width as the RTs (7ft 6in) and a total of 1,631 were built. They were, however, considered inferior to the RT and all were withdrawn from passenger service by November 1968. In their final years, several received early RT bodies with roof number boxes so that later RTL bodies could be placed on the more enduring RTs. A shortage of training buses in 1978 resulted in London Transport hiring several privately preserved RTs and RTLs, including RTL453 seen here leaving Chiswick Works.

until I holidayed abroad in 1967, Summer Holiday style, on a real London bus. This prompted me to obtain a PSV licence so that I could drive ex-London buses at weekends. My interest was further rekindled in 1973 when I moved to Harlington in Middlesex and RTs on route 140 passed my window. By then, I was aware that an era was ending and so I reached for my trusty Ilford Sportsman camera. Little did I know the extent to which the suburban and country bus scene would alter. It was not simply a case of substituting new buses for old, but something much more radical: the abandonment of old, established routes

Wot, no engine!

and the arrival of a wide variety of operators, vehicles and liveries in the name of reorganisation and deregulation.

There is history in these pages and an opportunity, I hope, to experience in living colour the atmosphere of yesterday's bus scene in the London area. The photographs are mine, unless otherwise stated, and particular appreciation goes to the unknown photographers whose original material has supplemented my collection. A thank you is also due to Judith Barnes for help with the text and to Bill Ballard and Julian Bowden for their photographic assistance.

My camera is now put away, but it is likely to reappear when the Routemaster's demise is imminent.

However, after many false alarms, and with the current refurbishment programme proceeding, the Routemaster in London service might actually outlive those who, like me, can recall its arrival in 1954! As for the other types featured in this book, many examples are enjoying an active retirement in preservation and a few are even still earning their keep with other operators. Long live these much loved buses!

Kevin R. McCormack
Ashtead, Surrey.
June 1992

Max Headroom

Before the advent of large capacity single-deckers, specially built double-deckers were used on routes with low bridges where passenger loadings required a larger vehicle than an average single-decker such as the RF. London Transport bought 20 low-height AEC Regents (RLHs) in 1950. These vehicles had originally been ordered by Midland General and were supplemented by a further 56 bought in 1952. The first of this second batch, RLH21, is seen in 1971 working as a courtesy bus for the Sheraton Hotel, near Heathrow. The reduced height — 13ft 6in instead of 14ft 6in — was achieved by fitting bench seats upstairs (clearly visible in this picture) and a sunken gangway — the latter providing many a downstairs passenger with a sore head!

Horseless carriage

Far left:
The first London bus service was started by George Shillibeer on 4 July 1829. The vehicle carried 22 passengers and was pulled by three horses abreast. In 1979, 25 Routemasters, with somewhat greater horsepower, were repainted in Shillibeer's original livery to commemorate the 150th anniversary. One of these repainted buses, RM2142, pauses in Chertsey Road, Lower Feltham, on route 237. This service had experienced a reversal of trends by being converted from one-person to conductor operation. Author's Collection

Last (Out)post

Left:
The RT bus served London for 40 years. Route 62, from Barking to Barkingside (the long way round), had the honour of being the last service, having earned a six-month reprieve to 7 April 1979. This was due to a narrow bridge at Chadwell Heath and the fact that RTs were at least six inches narrower than their successors. The problem was eventually solved by re-routing the 62. In this September 1978 scene, RT2293 heads away from Hainault Forest into New North Road.

7

Airbus

Left:
There were 700 RF single-deckers, dating from 1951-53, and 175 were modernised in the mid-1960s for continued Green Line operation. One such vehicle, RF47, is seen on route 727, a new service dating from May 1967 to link Heathrow and Gatwick airports. RFs were replaced by larger capacity coaches in 1971, shortly after the route was extended to Luton Airport. The roofboards were a feature of Green Line coaches from the start of services in 1930 until the early 1970s. The roof mountings on the RFs were then removed. Author's Collection

In a spin

Below left:
Starting life as a Green Line coach, RMC1518 was later repurchased by London Transport and is seen here demonstrating its abilities on the skid pan during the open day at Chiswick Works held in 1983 to commemorate the 50th anniversary of London Transport. Passengers were carried, but this was not a ride for the faint-hearted and the top deck was strictly out of bounds for safety reasons.

Shining Example

Right:
The anticipated demise of the red RTs by the mid-1970s was not to become reality and in 1975, when nearly 1,000 of the original class of 4,825 were still in service, a programme of recertification and long overdue repaints commenced. Stonebridge Park Garage have excelled themselves here with RT693. RM244 stands alongside on a trolleybus replacement route.

Old Timer

Left:

This auxiliary breakdown tender, numbered 832J, was originally a double-deck bus of 1933 vintage (numbered STL162) until fitted with a new van body in 1950. 832J had emerged from its garage in Neasden Underground Depot for a wash in preparation for its annual MOT test.

Seeing double

Below left:

In 1965, 43 long Routemaster coaches (classified RCLs) were delivered to London Transport for Green Line operation. With the end of crew operation in the early 1970s following the transfer of these services to London Country, the RCLs were relegated to bus work. In 1978-79 they were withdrawn and repurchased by London Transport. Several can now be found on sightseeing duties in London, some with open roofs. In June 1974, RCLs 2255 and 2257 were photographed on bus work at Crawley Garage. From the front the former coach Routemasters could be distinguished from their bus counterparts by the fitting of a different blind display and twin headlights. Author's Collection

Sunbath

Right:

In the winter of 1968, RT2071 basks in the sunshine at Southall Garage, southern terminus of the long-forgotten route 92B. 1968 was a significant year, marking the entry into service of the last Routemasters and the implementation of the 'Reshaping Programme', which introduced widespread one-person operation and caused many well-known routes to be renumbered. Southall was the local garage in my bus-spotting days and it was just round the corner, outside my father's golf club, that I was amazed to see my first diminutive GS-type — very much a stranger to those parts. Great excitement, particularly since, approaching from behind, the GS looked like an ordinary green RF.

Uptown bus

Left:
Where once they reigned supreme, RTs were becoming rare sights in Central London by the mid-1970s although a brief resurgence occurred when vehicle shortages prompted the transfer of RTs to services on which they had not operated for some years. Throughout this period, however, Catford Garage could be relied upon to produce some RTs for the premier route. At Oxford Circus RT3545, heading for Marylebone, passes RT1893 bound for Bricklayers Arms.

Top Box

Above:
Most of the RT fleet had bodies built by London Transport's normal suppliers — Park Royal and Weymann. However, shortly after delivery commenced in 1947, it was clear that the supply of bodies would not keep pace with chassis manufacture, thus prejudicing the withdrawal of time-expired prewar vehicles. To help overcome the shortfall, 300 bodies were built by Saunders on Anglesey, all of which were fitted with roof number boxes, a feature limited to the earliest Park Royal and Weymann vehicles. The Saunders RTs were nevertheless non-standard and although the bodies were interchangeable with those of the other builders during major overhaul, problems eventually arose over obtaining body panels and the premature withdrawal of this type became inevitable. In June 1970, during its last week of service, RT1371, from Hounslow Garage, enters Clare Road, Stanwell, on route 203A. This service was converted to one-person operation on 11 March 1972. The green radiator badge suggests that this red body had been married to a country bus chassis.

Blind spot

Far left:

London Country, like London Transport, had hoped to withdraw its last RTs by the mid-1970s. However, 19 still remained in service in 1976 and with an acute shortage of operational vehicles the company was obliged to recertify four of the best remaining RTs. The first, RT1018, re-entered service in April 1977 and its new NBC livery caused great interest. Unfortunately, the pristine appearance was marred by blinds which were not meant for RTs and which were also torn, causing the destination to be mis-spelt.

Deck and a half

Above left:

For many years, London Transport operated a London-Heathrow coach service on behalf of British European Airways (now part of British Airways). In 1952-53, 65 AEC Regal IV coaches were built with bodies designed by LT, which allowed passengers in the rear of the vehicle to be seated on a raised section above the luggage space. In 1966-67, these coaches were replaced by specially built front-entrance Routemasters, which had increased seating capacity and towed trailers containing passengers' luggage. Remarkably, one coach, MLL 740, was retained as a spare vehicle. When photographed leaving Terminal One at Heathrow in May 1969 it still wore the obsolete grey livery.

Feather in the cap

Below left:

London's smallest buses in the period covered by this book were 84 Guy 26-seaters built in 1953. Designated GS, they were one-person operated and worked on narrow or sparsely used Country Area routes. Features of this class included the Guy trademark, a Red Indian mascot on the bonnet, and a crash gearbox which required drivers to practice the art of 'double-declutching' to avoid grinding the gears. After less than 10 years' service, the GS began to be phased out but a handful survived to be taken over by London Country. GS operation finally ceased on 30 March 1972 when the 336A Rickmansworth-Loudwater Village service was withdrawn. This delightful route was notable for the fact that the GS did not return to the garage (Garston) each night but was taken home by the driver during the week, swopping with a second vehicle at the weekend. On the opposite side of London, GS56 is pictured in the summer of 1969 at Chelsham Garage, nursing two broken headlights.

Julian Bowden Collection

Semi-detached suburban

Far left:
Despite its grubby appearance, RT766 has been recently repainted and, unusually, is running without adverts (although the old ones seem to have been painted over). The vehicle is pictured heading down the North Circular Road in early 1976 en route from Golders Green to Chingford. Palmers Green Garage continued to turn out RTs on route 102 until April 1978.

Sylvan setting

Left:
The last red RFs (AEC Regal IVs) were due for withdrawal in 1977 but, because of the small inspection pits at Kingston Garage and a shortage of similar sized replacement vehicles, London Transport was forced to recertify 25 RFs for routes 218 and 219. These were eventually withdrawn on 30 March 1979, eight days before the last RTs. RF428, in modern livery with the LT bullseye, approaches Weybridge station during its last week of service.

Rose among thorns

Above:

RT3153 experiences the feminine touch from its driver at Kingston in the summer of 1973, flanked by two new Daimler Fleetlines (DMS600/611). The DMS class was unable to cope with London's demanding operational conditions and quickly fell from grace.

Misty morning

Right:

RMC1454 was one of 68 Routemaster coaches built in 1962 for Green Line services, preceding the larger RCL coaches. Both classes were introduced on routes where passenger numbers justified replacement of the single-deck RFs. However, the increase in the car-owning population during the 1960s rendered them redundant for this work and they were transferred to bus services. By 1978-79, one-person operation had brought about their demise on these duties too, and the majority were repurchased by London Transport from London Country (see the earlier photograph on p10). Author's Collection

Scenic diversion

Far left:
Road works in Argyle Road, West Ealing, caused the diversion of route 274 down The Avenue in the summer of 1976. RT4198 heads for Ealing Broadway on its journey from Hayes station. This service was converted from RT to one-person operation on 1 October 1977.

Foot on the gas

Left:
When London Transport's Country Bus and Coach Department was taken over by London Country on 1 January 1970 67% of the double-deck fleet was formed of RTs. Clearly these would not last long because of the company's commitment to 100% one-person operation. Nevertheless, RT overhauls continued, with London Country initially retaining LT's traditional Lincoln Green livery, but with yellow central relief band and lettering. In July 1974, however, RT4046 from Staines Garage has avoided a repaint and is seen passing the sadly extinct gas lamps which were a feature of the Englefield Green area. Route 441 from Staines to High Wycombe was officially converted to Routemaster operation in October 1972 although RTs did reappear occasionally. Readers may observe that this vehicle, and others featured in the book, have a tendency to wander across the road. This was because many of the photographs were taken with a minimum of planning and my car was parked at the kerb, just out of view!

Test bed

Right:

In July 1977, London Transport hired a 1959-built ex-Leeds double-decker from Dennis of Guildford in order to test the vehicle's experimental transmission and braking system. During its short stay in London, the Dennis was used on route 27, operating from Turnham Green Garage, where it proved popular with drivers. This busy traffic scene is in Chiswick High Road.

Last survivor

Far right:

London Country's RF202 outlived its red counterparts by a few months before suffering a gearbox failure in the summer of 1979. Consequently, there was no opportunity for a retirement party but, surprisingly, RF202 was repaired and repainted in the original Green Line livery applied to the modernised members of its class. It then continued to run for another 10 years on special duties such as this outing on the Ramblers' Service from Dorking on 17 August 1982. Seen here at Coldharbour, RF202 had several close encounters with Sunday drivers as it negotiated the narrow lanes on this route.

Rail link
Right:
RLH60 hurries down Kenton Road en route from Rayners Lane station to Northwick Park station with RT4266 in pursuit. Lowbridge route 230 became flat fare service H1 when it was converted to one-person operated single-deckers on 14 June 1969.

Seat of power
Below right:
The RT and its cousins, the RF and RLH, had standard AEC 9.6 litre engines with fluid flywheel and preselective gearbox. The latter was a great benefit to drivers because it enabled the vehicle to be kept in gear when stationary by holding it on the handbrake, although forgetting which gear had been preselected while the bus was in motion could have an unfortunate effect on the passengers! RT2794 enters Parliament Square on its journey from Euston to Tooting in September 1973, three months before RMs took over the route.
Author's Collection

What a relief

Above:

The prototype Routemaster coach, CRL4, entered service in October 1957, leading to the production of the RMCs in 1962. CRL4 was then modified to resemble the rest of the class more closely, becoming RMC4. Relegated from Green Line to bus services, it was withdrawn in 1979 but, like RF202, was restored by London Country to original Green Line livery for special events. In August 1982, it was pressed into service, complete with conductor and specially doctored blinds, to cope with extra traffic generated by a rail strike and is seen on this duty at Dorking Garage in somewhat undistinguished company.

Out of the blue

Left:
With other Heathrow hotels using modern coaches, it came as a surprise that the Sheraton Hotel should purchase two RTs in the 1970s, add doors and run them as courtesy buses between the hotel and London. RT4732 makes a colourful sight in the car park while its stable companion waits outside the hotel entrance.

Clothes show

Above:
Staines Garage in June 1974 with RMLs 2455/2413/2354 and RT4046 keeping company with 518J, formerly RLH44. The RLH, which displays the short-lived London Country logo, ended its working life as a mobile uniform store. Previously, it had made the unofficial last RLH public journey in London Country service on 31 July 1970.

27

Wide boy

Right:

When it became clear that AEC would be unable to produce sufficient buses after the war to replace London Transport's worn out fleet, an order was placed with Leyland Motors resulting in the RTL class and 500 RTWs. The 'W' signified that, at 8ft, they were six inches wider than the RT and RTL. Although not dissimilar from the front, the RTWs looked more unlike their counterparts from behind, mainly because of the positioning of the rear advertisements on the corner panels. The RTWs, like their RTL brothers, were unpopular with drivers, largely due to engine vibration and heavy steering, and LT began to withdraw them in the mid-1960s, after some 15 years of passenger service. The last RTWs ran in service in May 1966, 18 months before the RTLs were withdrawn, but some soldiered on as driver training buses until 1970. One such vehicle was RTW39, shown here at Acton Main Line station with its left-hand indicator illuminated. The positioning of the left and right-hand arrows together was thought to confuse following motorists and the nearside arrow was subsequently repositioned by the platform on the RTs that remained in service.

Long-distance runner

Below right:

In the days when double-deckers were still needed for Green Line relief duty, a seemingly empty RT3520 is in a jam at Hampton during the summer of 1974 while making its long trek from Windsor to Harlow. What the RT lacked in comfort, it would have made up for in terms of reliability, compared with the Green Line coaches of the period. Although these services no longer cross London, the Green Line name lives on after 62 years. The original company, Green Line Coaches Ltd, was formed in 1930 and was compulsorily purchased in 1933 when the London Passenger Transport Board was created.

Old soldier

Above:
D142, a Dennis of 1925 vintage, looks incongruous amongst the street clutter and road markings which epitomise modern London. This vehicle, which spent 39 years in a garden at Wickford before being rescued for preservation, causes some confusion as it stops outside Charing Cross station in the summer of 1980 while working vintage route 100.

29

Under the flightpath

Right:

Just a few hundred yards from the A4 Bath Road and yet newly-painted RT2168 could be meandering through a village instead of hurrying along High Street, Cranford, on its way to Heathrow in July 1975. Route 105 lost its RTs on 29 April 1978.

Red interloper

Far right:

London Country was quick to obliterate its London Transport parentage but links initially continued, as evidenced in this scene at Leatherhead Garage when route 71 still terminated there. With green RT4747 for company, red RT4480 advertises the London Transport Collection (now housed at Covent Garden), while its conductress, dressed in period costume, heads for the canteen.

Jersey cream

Right:

After less than five year's service in London, RTL1515 was one of an initial batch of eight RTLs sold to Jersey Motor Transport in March 1959. There it ran for a further 15 years before being repatriated for preservation. Jersey's green and cream livery suited these buses admirably.

Prodigal son

Far right:

As well as ordering non-standard vehicles from Saunders to make up the shortfall in new buses from standard suppliers, London Transport also ordered 120 RTs from Cravens in Sheffield. These were even less standard than the Saunders buses and LT resolved to dispose of them at the earliest opportunity. Thus, after only six to eight years of service, they were all withdrawn by 1957. Over 20 years later, privately preserved RT1499 was back in favour, having been hired by LT for driver training. Two unusual features — the extra windows on both decks and the upper deck appearing to be wider than the lower — are evident in this view of RT1499 leaving Chiswick Works in July 1978. But which is the stranger sight: the Craven RT or the boy taking four empty milk bottles for a walk?

Early bird

Far left:

In October 1977, when this photograph was taken, RT379 was numerically one of the oldest RTs in service, having entered service in March 1948. However, the system of swopping bodies and chassis at overhaul, because the bodies took longer to refurbish, has disguised RT379's real origins. A feature to note is the offside route number holder, which can be seen immediately to the left of the lower deck windows. The route number plates had been abolished in 1963-64 and in many cases the holders were replaced by plain panels. Notice also the very narrow panel above the driver's step which covers the space where the old-style trafficator arms were designed to be inserted. Only a few RTs carried these arms and they were quickly removed. RT379 is seen working from Plumstead Garage on route 122 prior to the conversion of this service on 22 April 1978.

Worse for Wear

Left:

During the 1970s, the repainted RTs naturally attracted the attention of photographers but, in fact, many of the class looked distinctly shabby. RT2272 is a typical example, as it proceeds up London Road, near Thornton Heath, on route 119A in the summer of 1977. Surprisingly, it has managed to retain its triangular radiator badge but one wonders for how long, since these badges were popular souvenirs.

Blue bird

Far left:

Continental Pioneer's RF506, an ex-London Transport red bus which I drove many times, looks very smart as it receives attention in Richmond Yard during the summer of 1979. LT had abandoned route 235, from Richmond station to Richmond Hill, in 1966 and Pioneer took it over until 27 September 1980. The service was then covered by a diversion of route 71. The benefits of the RF's preselective gearbox were much appreciated when undertaking a blind reverse turn at the top of the hill, since the alternative bus, a Ford with a manual gearbox, caused muscle ache!

Capital transport

Left:

The 140 was one of the longest routes in London, joining Heathrow Airport with Mill Hill, and seemed likely at one time to be the last RT-operated service. In fact, it was the fourth last, being converted to Routemaster operation unexpectedly on 15 July 1978. Eight years earlier, Harrow Weald Garage was still able to muster the occasional Saunders-bodied roofbox-fitted RT, by then nearing the end of its career. RT3186, seen here at Heathrow Airport Central, carries an intermediate blind designed for the rear of the bus. It is interesting to note that the blind predates the change from upper to lower case lettering, which occurred in 1961 to improve clarity.

Airport express

Above:

MLL 740, the last one-and-a-half deck airline coach in service, has discarded the grey livery shown earlier for the new BEA salmon colour, having missed the intervening blue and white livery of the 1966-69 period. Seen here in June 1970 passing the Terminal One car park at Heathrow, the vehicle looks resplendent but its appearance was subsequently marred by the obliteration of the BEA crest on the front. MLL 740 outlived the other 64 members of the class by six years and was withdrawn in May 1973. It is now preserved at Cobham Bus Museum in Surrey.

Smart Guy

Right:

GS56 looks remarkably tidy in its London Transport livery following its sale to Bickers of Coddenham, Suffolk, on 5 September 1969. Admittedly, the Guy's appearance is not enhanced by the application of an advertisement across the emergency exit but the LT bullseye is a pleasing feature. The similarity of the bodywork of the GS and RF, when viewed from the rear, is clearly evident. GS56 served London Transport for almost 16 years, operating from Amersham, Dunton Green and Chelsham garages.
Julian Bowden Collection

Short lived splendour

Far left:
Fresh from the paint shop and devoid of adverts, RT848 stands in Bath Road, Hartlington, beside Heathrow Airport, in summer 1975. Sad to believe that, within a short time, this fine vehicle would suffer the fate of the RTs on the last page and become a 'turnover' vehicle for trainee recovery gangs.

Leaving the stage

RT3461, newly outshopped for London Country in National Bus Company leaf green, descends Sanderstead Hill en route for West Croydon in May 1977. Within four months this vehicle was taken out of passenger service and relegated to training duties.

City bus

Above:

London was not the only city served by London Transport. St Albans also came within the LT area and this is where this September 1967 photograph of RF603, standing alongside RT4050, was taken. Although St Albans was firmly established in LT's green Country Area, evidence of the fact that it was also reached by red Central Area buses can be seen from the reflection in the RF's windscreen of an RT on route 84. RF603 is operating route 391, which plied between Sandridge and Tyttenhanger, a world away from the hustle and bustle of the big city. Author's Collection

Whither Sherwood Forest?

Right:

Newly-painted RT1063, still free of adverts, prepares to leave North Street Garage, Romford, on 15 June 1975 in search of Robin Hood and Little John at Brentwod. Route 247 was converted to one-person operation on 24 April 1976 using small BL-type single-deckers. Author's Collection

Art decker

Far left:
During the 1970s, all-over advertising became popular and several Routemasters were decorated. One of the most attractive liveries was carried by RM783, seen here in the winter of 1972 at Stamford Hill on route 149, bound for Liverpool Street. Author's Collection

Village green

Left:
RT4721 negotiates the pleasant backwater of Norwood Green, on the Southall/Heston border, with a short rush-hour working on route 120 in mid-1976. RTs survived on this route until 28 January 1978, outliving the diseased elm trees in the background.

Colour blind

Right:

Although red and green buses frequently met, it was rare for them to operate on one another's services. However, a shortage of red lowbridge RLHs for route 230 (now H1) caused London Transport to borrow from its Country Area department. During the final period of the route's existence green RLH27 was regularly used and is seen here at Rayners Lane with RT4262 on route 98B. On the RT, the panel covering the aperture for the nearside trafficator can be seen between the cab and the saloon.

Shattered

Far right:

At first glance, RT4756 looks resplendent as it stands at Raynes Park in the autumn of 1973 on route 77A, but, judging by the state of its windscreen, it will not be returning to King's Cross. Author's Collection

One and only

Left:

This vehicle might have been the first in a fleet of front-entrance, rear-engined Routemasters. However, quality costs extra and London Transport was forced instead to invest in standard off-the-shelf products, which turned out to be a false economy. FRM1 entered service on 23 June 1967 and, after trials on various routes, was sent to Potters Bar Garage in October 1973 to operate route 284, a service which required only one vehicle. After an accident in 1976, it was moved to the Round London Sightseeing Tour, where it ended its operational career. It is now preserved as part of the London Transport Museum collection.

Wearing of the green

Above:

The majority of the 700-strong RF class were built for Green Line coach work. Of the remainder, red Central Area buses outnumbered green Country buses but several of the latter still remained when London Country was created in 1970. Twenty-four years old when photographed at Chelsham Garage in the summer of 1977, RF684 was one of the last vehicles to remain in the traditional Lincoln green.

Motorway madness

Left:

RT2615 in overtaking mode on the M4 Airport spur as it heads for Shepiston Lane and Cherry Lane Cemetery on one of the two special Sunday workings of route 140. A stirring sight, considering the bus was nearly 30 years old and would be replaced by RMs in the following month.

Provincial intruder

Above:

BM8, an ex-Midland Red D9, waits outside Putney Bridge Underground station. Hired to London Transport in the early 1980s for the Round London Sightseeing Tour, it is seen here on a railway emergency service, while essential engineering work is carried out on the British Rail-owned stretch of the District Line to Wimbledon.

Going to the zoo

Far left:
Another of London Transport's longest routes was the 65 which ran originally from Ealing to Leatherhead, but was later cut back to Chessington Zoo. A mobile canteen for crews used to stand at the Argyle Road terminus. Newly-painted RT4165 pulls out of Eaton Rise on a short working to Norbiton Church in the autumn of 1974. This route was converted to RM operation on 19 October 1975 and has since undergone considerable change, being curtailed to Ealing Broadway-Kingston and transferred to an independent operator, Armchair.

Industrial revolution

Left:
Routes 65 and 97 were the local services of my childhood, but RT472 has left behind the leafy avenues of Ealing as it crosses the railway bridge in Windmill Road, Brentford, heading for the Half Acre. The 97 reminds me of happy days at Ruislip Lido, and the excitement of spotting my first green RT there; but it was a long haul on the summer Sunday extension. Change came with the arrival of one-person operation on 30 November 1968 when the E2 flat-fare service took over the Greenford-Brentford section. However, the introduction of the E2 and the neighbouring E1 and E3 services brought unexpected compensation in the form of two new RT-operated services into Ealing — the 273 and 274.

Family likeness

Above:

This line up of RT2137 (route 176) and RMs 2166, 2172 and 2218 at Willesden Garage shows the similarities between these two vehicle types which enabled the Routemaster to assume so readily the role of the traditional London bus previously occupied by the RT. The RM, however, was wider than the RT (8ft rather than 7ft 6in) and longer (27ft 6in rather than 26ft), increasing passenger capacity from 56 to 64.

Mixed parentage

Right:

The blue radiator badge on this RT suggests that its chassis previously carried a red body. In the summer of 1973, RT4117 approaches Ewell village on a short working of the Kingston-Redhill 406 service.

RFs rule OK

Left:
Single-deck RFs monopolise the bus park at Uxbridge station in May 1973. Windsor's RF301 was originally RF520 from the same 1953-built batch as red RF598 behind. Both were once green, but RF520 was converted into a Green Line coach in 1956 and was consequently renumbered.

Triplets

Above:
Chessington Zoo in the summer of 1973 and RT1538 on route 71 heads for Richmond, passing between RT4344, on a short working of route 468 to Epsom, and RT3964 waiting to leave for Ealing, Argyle Road, on route 65.

Generation gap

Above:

Bristol BLs replaced RFs on many of the Kingston routes. In the spring of 1977, BL47 on route 216 rests outside the former Staines West railway station in the company of RF545 on route 218, while RM997 prepares to leave for Hounslow bus station on route 117. The RF still retains the underlined fleet name, London Transport. This was introduced in 1933 when the London Passenger Transport Board was created and perpetuated by its successor, the Nationalised London Transport Executive, which assumed control of London's buses (under the British Transport Commission) in 1948.

Allsorts

Right:

Spring 1972, and four vehicle types are on offer at Hounslow bus station. Prospective passengers seeking reliable transport can choose between a trip to Shepherds Bush Green on RM1134, Richmond courtesy of RF522 or the White Hart at Yeading on RT2710. The Merlin on route 116 wisely keeps its doors closed.

Home bird

Left:

RLH14, seen here leaving Chertsey in July 1969, was built at Weymann's works at nearby Addlestone in June 1950 and spent its entire 20 years of service based at Addlestone Garage. The offending bridge, which required the use of lowbridge buses on route 436A, was in Chertsey Lane, Staines.

Well-groomed Green Line

Below:

Eighty-five RTs were allocated to Green Line services in the 1950s and 1960s and were distinguishable from normal Country buses by the absence of posters and by the application of Green Line markings. In July 1969, RT3647 from Garston Garage finds employment on bus work near Rickmansworth. Rear wheel discs were fitted to virtually all classes of London bus, but were removed in 1971-72.

Last stronghold

Left:
Barking was the last garage to operate RTs, using them on routes 62 and 87. The latter, from Rainham to Harold Hill, became RM operated in October 1978, although RTs still occasionally appeared until the 62 was converted. On that fateful day, 7 April 1979, crowds thronged round Barking Garage, the press and TV cameramen were there, and the RTs had a send-off to be remembered. The farewell was scheduled for the previous weekend until it was realised that this would coincide with the retirement of the RFs.

Sixteen year reprieve

Above:
Routemasters were in continuous production from 1959 to 1968 and after the end of the trolleybus conversion programme in 1962, they began to replace the RTs and the Leylands. The first garages scheduled for conversion to RM operation were Harrow Weald and Edgware, but union opposition led to a change of policy involving the conversion of individual routes rather than complete garages. Ironically, as late as the spring of 1978, when this photograph was taken, Harrow Weald Garage was still full of RTs, although 27 years of use on route 140 was shortly to end. Smart RT1850 fraternises with, amongst others, RTs 4171 and 1171. The former carries the plain fleet name with no underlining, which was latterly applied to many RTs. Unlike some RFs, however, none was ever destined to wear the white LT bullseye.

This little piggy ...

Far left:
Market day in May 1973 and the residents of Stanwell Moor are provided with their twice weekly service to Staines, courtesy of route 444 and RF247. A comparison between this bus and RF660 seen earlier illustrates the subtle livery change from cream to yellow relief implemented by London Country and the attempts to obliterate the London Transport bullseye on the front. On the RFs the LT bullseye gave discreet access to the radiator.

Entente uncordiale

Left:
RTL1050 visits Paris in August 1967 while returning from a Double-Decker Club holiday in the south of France. The RTL created considerable attention, particularly among the gendarmes when it was parked under the Eiffel Tower! With its roof badly dented by overhanging trees, RTL1050 became an obvious candidate for subsequent conversion to an open-topper.

Chequered career

Left:

ST922 was one of a batch of 191 AEC Regents with outside staircases supplied in 1930-31 to Thomas Tilling. Acquired by the new London Passenger Transport Board in 1933 when this organisation took over 61 independent operators, ST922 was first withdrawn before the war, but was then reinstated until finally retired from public service in 1947. Even then, its working life was not yet over for it was converted into a mobile canteen, carrying the number 693J. It was eventually discarded by London Transport in 1954 and lay in a scrapyard near Hitchin for many years until being rescued in 1971. Rebuilt and recertified for public service, this proud veteran ventured back on to the streets of London, operating on vintage route 100. In May 1978, ST922 was pictured at Trafalgar Square, emerging from Whitehall.

House of Windsor

Above:

RF55, dating from 1951, was built as a Green Line coach but later relegated to bus work. It is seen standing at Windsor Garage in June 1973, along with RML2354. The small window half way along the body distinguishes this 72-seat Routemaster from the standard 64-seat version. The two vehicles sandwiched between the RF and RML represent a generation of bus which is best forgotten. The substantial brick-built garage is also no more. Author's Collection

Pondering the end

Left:
In the twilight of their careers, RTs 948 and 3472 stand at Enfield Garage in the summer of 1972. Author's Collection

Time Warp

Above:
This could be a mid-1960s scene as 'modernised' RF202 enters Staines on the Harlow-Windsor route 718. But in fact the photograph was taken on 5 December 1981 when the RF worked two round trips from Victoria to mark the retirement of the last 'clippie' at Staines Garage.

Family Outing

Left:

Although frequently employed on the Round London Sightseeing Tour, RMF2791 also undertook less prestigious duties, particularly when, as seen here, I took it home! Despite the red livery, this vehicle was never owned by London Transport but originated with Northern General, the only provincial operator of the Routemaster. These buses, like the BEA examples, had front entrances fitted with doors, a feature which was confined, in LT's fleet, to FRM1 and RM1254. The latter was hired to BEA and later sold to Northern General. Northern General disposed of its Routemaster fleet in 1979 and although LT bought a few, they were never used.

Preparing for take-off

Above:

The date is 20 May 1973 and RF379, built in 1952, stands at Uxbridge on route 223 bound for Heathrow Airport. This was a rare case of a conversion from RT to RF operation, which occurred on 16 January 1971. RML2439 stands behind, waiting to leave for Abbots Langley on route 347A. On the right is a standard LT tubular bus shelter: an excellent structure on which to practice gymnastics!

Rainy day blues

Above:

This May 1964 scene at Clapham Common shows RM1357 in original condition passing blue RT4265. The latter represents an early sale of a standard RT and an example of an old roof box body being placed on a later chassis.

Driver's pet

Right:

Route 94 was served by Catford and Bromley garages and became the ante-penultimate RT-operated service, although latterly shared with RMs, as shown here. The RTs' 28-year reign ended on 25 August 1978 and one month earlier RT449 cruises down Southborough Lane, Petts Wood. Some bus drivers on this route were proud to be photographed with their old faithfuls and would slow down or pull away gradually to facilitate a good shot.

Day at the races

Left:

Red RT833 and green RT4755 meet at Tattenham Corner, Epsom Downs, in the spring of 1973. Although construction of RTs ceased in November 1954, some were stored until 1959 due to falling passenger demand. RT4755 entered service in April 1958.

Unadorned

Above:

Standing at Dartford Garage in June 1974, modernised RF65 must be lamenting the loss of its Green Line two-tone colour scheme in favour of the NBC corporate livery then being enforced on London Country.

Party invitation

Right:

RT3234 passes through South Harrow oblivious of the fact that, within a month, it would be decorated with Union Jack balloons and streamers for the last RT journey from Harrow Weald Garage.

Open-topper

Far right:

The OMs were a fleet of seven ex-Midland Red D9s, which were deroofed before being hired to London Transport for the Round London Sightseeing Tour. The RF-type bullseye attached to the radiator is clearly visible as OM2 proceeds down Haymarket in May 1980.

Full-up inside

Right:

This is not a case of the residents of Richmond finding an ingenious way of increasing the seating capacity of 56, but a holiday trip to the south of France in August 1968. I spent many happy days perched on the front of RTL1023 with the acquiescence of the gendarmes, who seemed resigned to the fact that this was how the British normally travelled by bus!

War veteran

Far right:

The RTs featured so far in this book were all built between 1947 and 1954. However, the first 151 members of the class entered service between 1939 and 1942 and could be distinguished from the postwar version by the curved line to the base of the cabside window and windscreen and by a rear roof box. By May 1955 (Central Area) and September 1957 (Country Area), the whole class had been withdrawn from passenger service and after use on miscellaneous duties, all were retired by the early 1960s except for two which remained in the service fleet. These were RT1, mounted on a later chassis and now thankfully preserved, and RT106. The latter, ominously renumbered 1036TV, became a turnover vehicle for trainee recovery crews. Two lifting holes can be seen in the upper deck. The vehicle is pictured at Stonebridge Park in February 1970 at the end of an arduous life spanning nearly 30 years.

Down and out

Above:
Another depressing scene at Stonebridge Park as the underside of an overturned RT is revealed.

RF Quintet

Back cover:
Kingston Bus Station still retains its period atmosphere today, but the line up of RFs in this April 1975 scene is history. RFs 537, 515 and 505 are nearest the camera.